World of Islam

Islamic-Jewish Relations Before 1947

MASON CREST PUBLISHERS
PHILADELPHIA

World of Islam

Islamic-Jewish Relations Before 1947

TANYA SKLAR

Editorial Consultants: Foreign Policy Research Institute, Philadelphia, PA

Mason Crest Publishers
370 Reed Road
Broomall, PA 19008
www.masoncrest.com

Copyright © 2010 by Mason Crest Publishers. All rights reserved.
Printed and bound in the United States of America.

First printing

1 3 5 7 9 8 6 4 2

Library of Congress Cataloging-in-Publication Data

Sklar, Tanya.
   Islamic-Jewish relations before 1947 / Tanya Sklar.
      p. cm. — (World of islam)
   ISBN 978-1-4222-1361-2 (hardcover) — ISBN 978-1-4222-1364-3 (pbk.)
   1. Islam—Relations—Judaism. 2. Judaism—Relations—Islam. I. Title.

   BP173.J8S6 2006
   297.2'8209—dc22
                                2009023215

Photo Credits: 7: Used under license from Shutterstock, Inc.; 8: Library of Congress; 10: Used under license from Shutterstock, Inc.; 13: Used under license from Shutterstock, Inc.; 14: Library of Congress; 16: Michael Di Biase/Saudi Aramco World/Padia; 20: © OTTN Publishing, LLC; 21: Used under license from Shutterstock, Inc.; 23: Collection of Tanya Sklar; 26: Library of Congress; 28: U.S. Navy photo by Photographer's Mate 1st Class Arlo K. Abrahamson/DoD; 30: Used under license from Shutterstock, Inc.; 32: © 2009 Jupiterimages Corporation; 34: Library of Congress; 39: Used under license from Shutterstock, Inc.; 48: Department of Defense; 42: © 2009 Jupiterimages Corporation; 44: Library of Congress; 47: (top) UN Photo/MB, (inset) © Kluger Zoltan/The State of Israel; 50: Used under license from Shutterstock, Inc.; 55: Used under license from Shutterstock, Inc.; 58: Used under license from Shutterstock, Inc.

Tanya Sklar is a research assistant at The Global Research in International Affairs (GLORIA) Center. Tanya holds a BA Degree in International Relations and Counter Terrorism from the Raphael Recanati International School at the Hertzlia Interdisciplinary Center, Israel.

World of Islam

Table of Contents

Jews and Early Islam

Historically, relations between Muslims and Jews have been complicated and variable. From the early decades of Islam, in the seventh century CE, the large Jewish minorities across the Middle East experienced both persecution and periods of relative coexistence with the dominant Muslim population.

The Beginnings of Islam

Muhammad, Islam's founding prophet, viewed himself as a messenger of God whose role was to create a large and powerful monotheistic religion with a united community of followers. Born in 570 CE in Mecca, an important town on the western Arabian Peninsula in what is today Saudi Arabia, Muhammad was orphaned as a young boy. He was raised by an uncle. By the time Muhammad was in his twenties, he had worked as a shepherd

An ornate niche inside the Prophet's Mosque in Medina, Saudi Arabia. During the 620s, Muhammad established the first mosque and created the first Islamic community in Medina.

and trader, traveling to Syria and Yemen with camel caravans that carried goods to regional commercial centers. Throughout his travels, Muhammad would have become acquainted with diverse cultures and religions, including Judaism and Christianity.

Around the age of 40, Muhammad became discontented with his life in Mecca. He often found retreat in caves in the surrounding mountains, where he meditated on the deeper meaning of life. According to Islamic belief, it was in the cave that he first received a revelation from Allah (God), delivered by the angel Gabriel. The angel told Muhammad to proclaim Allah's words. Over the next 22 years, Muslims believe, Muhammad received

As a young man, Muhammad guided caravans like this one between Mecca and Damascus. During his travels, he was exposed to practitioners of many religious faiths, including Christians, Jews, and Zoroastrians.

more revelations. These were eventually written down in the Qur'an, Islam's holy scriptures.

During Muhammad's time, Jews traveled through many lands as merchants and craftsmen. Many were drawn to commercial centers on the Arabian Peninsula, where caravans conducted trade with neighboring countries. These commercial centers included Yathrib, an oasis town located about 200 miles north of Mecca. There were three main Jewish tribes in Yathrib. These were the Banu Nadir, the Banu Qaynuqa, and the Banu Qurayza, who lived among the larger pagan community.

In 622, Muhammad and a few hundred of his followers—the totality of the early Muslim community—were forced to flee Mecca in the face of persecution there. They went to Yathrib, which would later be renamed Medina ("City of the Prophet") in Muhammad's honor.

Early on, Muhammad needed to gain the support of the Jewish tribes living in Medina, whose relationships with one another were frequently contentious. His plan was to create a community constitution. The agreement, which became known as the "Constitution of Medina," gave certain responsibilities and rights to Muslims and to Jews. For example, it committed both groups to the mutual defense of Medina—an important consideration for Muhammad, given the Meccans' ongoing hostility toward Muslims. According to the constitution, Jews—who, like Muslims, practiced a monotheistic religion—would be free to worship as they chose.

Initially, Muhammad managed to establish good relationships with many of the Jews of Medina and surrounding areas. However, differences and tensions between followers of the two faiths soon emerged. As the Muslim community grew in size, it gained in influence. Eventually, Muhammad and his followers were powerful enough to exile the Banu Qaynuqa and

Banu Nadir tribes from Medina after recurring conflicts with the Muslim community.

The Qurayza Massacre

In 627, when a Meccan army laid siege to Medina, the Jewish Banu Qurayza tribe did not come to the aid of the Muslims. After the Meccans abandoned the siege, Muhammad accused the Banu Qurayza of breaching the Medina constitution by aiding the Muslims' enemies. The following year, Muslim forces isolated the Banu Qurayza, laying siege to their fortress in Medina.

The Kaaba—the square black structure in the center of Mecca's Grand Mosque—is considered by Muslims to be the holiest shrine in the world. Muhammad and his followers were at war with the Meccans from 622 to 630, when the Muslims were able to conquer Mecca. Muhammad removed the idols from the Kaaba and rededicated the structure to worship of Allah.

After nearly a month, the Banu Qurayza surrendered under the promise of fair arbitration. The leader of an Arab tribe, Sa'd ibn Muadh, was chosen to judge the matter. He decided that all the adult male members of the Banu Qurayza should be executed. Muhammad approved the decision, and an estimated 700 to 900 tribesmen were beheaded in Medina's main market square. The tribe's women and children were sold into slavery or given to Muhammad's companions as gifts.

Muhammad justified the act, referring to it as God's decree. According to the Qur'an, "Allah hath cursed them [the Jews] for their disbelief" (4: 46). Immediately after the massacre, the property and riches of the tribe were divided among the Muslims of Medina.

Period of Conquest

By 630, Muhammad and the Muslims had triumphed in the conflict with the Meccans, marching unopposed into the city. Many Meccans converted to Islam. Muhammad proceeded to destroy all the polytheistic idols in Mecca's Kaaba shrine, effectively suppressing paganism in Mecca.

Over the next two years, Muslim control over the Arabian Peninsula was consolidated. Muhammad advocated spreading the Islamic faith further, into non-Muslim states. In 632, he died unexpectedly while in the midst of preparations for a military campaign against the Byzantine Empire.

Under Muhammad's successors, the four so-called rightly guided caliphs—who acted as political and religious rulers—Arab armies did indeed expand the territory under the control of Islam. Between 632 and 661, when the fourth caliph was assassinated, Muslim armies launched successful attacks against the Byzantine Empire as well as the Persian Sassanid Empire. The territory they conquered became part of a growing Islamic empire.

During the seventh century, the majority of Middle Eastern Jewry had lived within the Byzantine Empire, whose territory included what are now Syria, Egypt, Israel, Jordan, and Lebanon. Since biblical times, significant numbers of Jews had been residing in cities like Aleppo, under various rulers.

The remains of a Byzantine fortification in the city of Thessaloniki, modern-day Greece. The Byzantine, or Eastern Roman, Empire was under continual pressure from Muslim armies after the seventh century CE.

Byzantine policy dictated that all non-Christians, including the Jews, were burdened with high taxes and strict religious restrictions. There was tremendous pressure to convert to Christianity to avoid religious persecution.

Groups of Jews also remained in Persia, suffering equally from the stringent rule of the Sassanid Empire, the Byzantine Empire's greatest rival. Neither of these empires had anticipated the severity of the threat from Arab forces. Moreover, they were exhausted from decades of war against each other, which greatly facilitated the victory of the Muslims.

Holy War

In Islam, a soldier who dies in a *jihad* (a holy war to spread the Islamic faith) is considered a martyr and will reap eternal reward. For the Arabs, therefore, efforts to expand the Islamic empire involved not just the strategic conquest of territory but a divine mandate to increase the *umma* (Muslim community).

Ruins of the imperial palace at Ctesiphon, once the capital of the Persian Sassanid Empire. Arab forces captured the city in 637, completing their conquest of Persia by 644.

Ruling newly conquered territories presented a variety of difficulties in the early decades of the Islamic empire. To begin, the Arabs numbered far fewer than the peoples they now controlled. Moreover, they came largely from tribal backgrounds and lacked the administrative and commercial skills needed to manage a complex state. Thus they needed to secure the cooperation (or at least the acquiescence) of the non-Muslim majorities in conquered territories. For this reason, forced religious conversion was often not a priority during the early decades of Islam's rapid expansion. Muslim rulers recognized that conversion to their faith could take place over a longer period.

The Regulation of Jewish Life

A policy evolved for the treatment of non-Muslims in Muslim-ruled lands. In principle, no polytheistic religions would be tolerated at all, while Christians and Jews would be considered as *dhimmis*. This new social status, unique to the Islamic faith, was based on a verse from the Qur'an: "Fight against those who believe not in Allah, nor in the Last Day, nor forbid that which has been forbidden by Allah and His Messenger, and those who acknowledge not the religion of truth among the People of the Scripture, until they pay the *jizya* [a special tax] with willing submission, and feel themselves subdued" (9:29).

The dhimmi concept, which remains part of Islamic law to this day, was a relationship in which Jews and Christians would receive "protection" from the Muslim authorities in exchange for their acceptance of second-class status, as manifested by their payment of a special tax. Crucially, the jizya was lower than the taxes Jews and Christians had paid under the Byzantine and Persian rulers. Aside from the political and strategic benefits—namely, reducing the chances that the non-Muslim majorities in conquered provinces would revolt—the dhimmi policy served a

Gold coin issued by the Umayyad caliph Abd al-Malik, and struck at the Damascus mint around 693. Jews and Christians living in Muslim lands were permitted to keep their faiths, as long as they swore allegiance to the Muslim rulers and paid a special tax, called the *jizya*.

religious goal as well. In the long run, it encouraged conversion to Islam.

While dhimmis were granted certain freedoms, such as the ability to practice their chosen religion, mainly in private, they were still viewed as an occupied population to be "brought low" (Qu'ran 2:61, 9:29). The public sphere would be a completely Islamic environment. Thus, dhimmis were prohibited from building or repairing places of worship without the permission of the Muslim leaders. Their places of worship could not be as high as mosques; bells and the public display of crosses on churches were banned for Christians. Dhimmis would be forced to wear distinctive clothing that differed from that of the Muslims so they could be clearly distinguished and the limits on their behavior enforced.

Economic incentives were also used to encourage voluntary conversion. Muslims did not pay the jizya, and an act of conversion would instantly do away with all the limits to daily life and extra taxes anyone had to pay. Moreover, all barricades to one's career and commercial prospects would disappear.

Another technique for encouraging conversion was the creation of "private towns," known as *amsars*. These upper-class towns only welcomed Muslim residents. The amsar system proved successful, resulting in widespread conversion to the Islamic faith and thus the strengthening of the Muslim empire. Before long, there was a high demand for amsars, and several new cities were built.

People of the Book

At the same time, Jews and Christians were classified as *Ahl al-Kitab* ("People of the Book") by the Qur'an. On one hand, Jews and Christians were given lower status than Muslims, but they were also seen as superior to people who were not monotheists. The phrase *Ahl al-Kitab* refers to the fact that a religion also had a written holy text, though these texts were deemed to have been superseded by the Qur'an. (Later a third group was added to the category *Ahl al-Kitab*: Zoroastrians, who had great influence in the conquered territories of the Persian Empire.)

Presumably, the authorities in the Islamic empire would protect Jews (and other dhimmis) who were being harassed or extorted by individual Muslims or groups not authorized by the state. Jews were exempt from military service, which was an advantage to them (though the rulers also saw this as a sign of their lower status). Yet they were also not allowed to have weapons, even for personal protection, which means that they would be helpless if attacked by others.

They could pursue their livelihoods unhindered, and in some ways conditions were improved over what they had lived with under the previous regimes. Since the Jews were uninterested in meddling in politics—which they saw as a terribly dangerous thing to do—restrictions in this area did not bother them. Yet they could not serve as witnesses in Muslim (that is, state) law courts, which put them at a tremendous disadvantage in any dispute with a Muslim, making them helpless to protect themselves legally.

If physical repression was rare, it was because the system worked well. The Jews were never involved in revolts. Moreover, in contrast to European Christianity, the Muslims had a number of different non-Muslim groups to contend with, while in Europe Jews were the only non-Christian minority and had all the forces of power and prejudice focused on them.

In places, Islam's holy texts enjoin believers to treat People of the Book justly. For example, in the Hadith (collected sayings and traditions of Muhammad and his close companions), Muhammad warns, "He who wrongs a Jew or a Christian will have myself as his indicter on the Day of Judgment." However, in numerous other places in Islamic holy writings, Jews are portrayed as "the vilest of creatures" and people who "will burn in hell fire" (Qur'an 4:55, 98:6). And during the Middle Ages, debates among Muslims led to the eventual end of the limited rights Jews were entitled to as People of the Book.

The Consolidation of Islam's Empire

By 644, the first two caliphs, Abu Bakr and Umar ibn al-Khattab, had succeeded in conquering Syria, the land of Palestine, Egypt, Mesopotamia, Persia, and even territories as far away as the Indus River in what is today Pakistan. At one time, some sources suggest, Umar decreed that all the Jews and non-Muslims be removed from the empire in order to preserve Muslim sovereignty. If so, however, this policy was never implemented.

After the assassination of Ali ibn Abi Talib, the fourth caliph, in 661, an Islamic ruling dynasty was established. Under the Umayyads, who established their capital in Damascus, regulations concerning the dhimmis were tightened and changed periodically.

In the eighth century, for example, an Umayyad sultan made it compulsory for Jews and Christians to have special signs above the entrances of their homes in order to distinguish themselves from Muslims. Similarly, non-Muslims were forced to wear colored sashes. The problem, of course, was not with the clothing itself. Because they were easily identified, Jews and other dhimmis could be singled out for mistreatment by any Muslim.

The Muslim Conquest of Spain

The year 711 marked the beginning of the Muslim conquest of the Iberian Peninsula—modern-day Spain and Portugal. Muslim forces, led by the Berber leader Tariq ibn Ziyad, landed on the southern Spanish coastline near Gibraltar. Soon southern Spain was annexed to the Muslim empire. Historians, however, believe that it was only in the 10th century, with the arrival of the leader Abd al-Rahman, that Islam truly took hold in the Iberian Peninsula.

From the late sixth century until the time of the Muslim invasion, Spain had been governed by the Visigoths, who were known for the strict religiosity of their reign. Under the

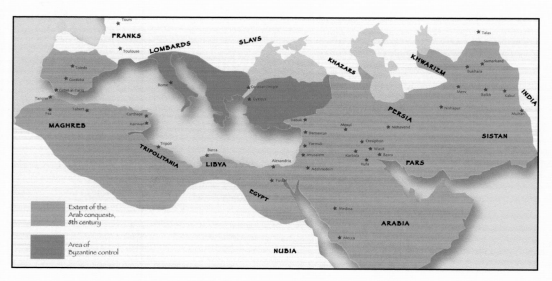

This map shows the extent of the Arab Islamic empire. By the middle of the eighth century, a large percentage of the world's Jewish population lived in lands ruled by Muslims.

Catholic rule of the Visigoths, Spanish Jewry had suffered discrimination and serious persecution. Many Jews were forced to flee Spain or convert to Christianity, in many cases in order to save their lives.

For centuries, Spain had been populated by large Jewish communities, which were situated mainly in the south. The residents of these communities worked as traders and merchants in thriving cities. As the Muslim conquest reached Granada, Seville, and Córdoba, Muslims and Jews established ties. Spanish Jewry, which had suffered under the Catholics, embraced the change in rule and welcomed the Muslim leadership.

The Muslim invasion brought improvements to Spanish Jewry, if for no other reason than for the emerging stability and the uniting of many small feudal holdings, which facilitated trade. The 10th and 11th centuries were considered a golden age in Muslim-controlled Spain, and Jews too benefited. They were permitted to reside in selected areas across southern Spain, whose large and prosperous cities were centers of commerce, arts, and the sciences.

Though life for Spanish Jewry improved in many respects under Muslim rule, they still faced persecution. In 1066, more than 1,500 Jewish

The Court of the Lions is part of the Alhambra, a palace-fortress built by the Muslim rulers of the southern Iberian Peninsula. The Moors—Arab and Berber Muslims from North Africa—conquered much of the peninsula during the eighth century CE.

families were put to death in Granada. Joseph ibn Nagrela, a Jew who had served the Muslim king of Granada, was suspected of a coup attempt and was crucified.

Nagrela's earlier life is often used as an example of a "golden age" of tolerance for Jews, but what happened to him in the end is frequently ignored or downplayed in such accounts. The point is, however, that while Jews could do well in Muslim-ruled countries, they always faced the threat of downfall and persecution, in large part because their very higher status had no legitimacy in the code governing Muslim society.

The Rambam

Moses Maimonides, also known in Hebrew as the Rambam, was a medieval Jewish physician, philosopher, and writer famous for his interpretations of many Jewish scriptures (perhaps most importantly those of the Jewish book of law known as the Mishneh Torah). Maimonides was originally from Córdoba, but in 1148 he and his family fled Spain after the Almohad dynasty had taken power. The Berber Almohads imposed a strict interpretation of Islam, especially concerning the dhimmis. The regime forced Jews to convert to Islam, leave the country, or face death. Like many others, Maimonides chose to leave. He eventually settled in Egypt, where he came to hold an important position in the administration of the Fatimid dynasty rulers and was respected by Muslims and Jews alike. (The once-unified Islamic empire had by this time fragmented into a variety of Islamic states.)

In 1172, Maimonides wrote his "Epistle to the Jews in Yemen," addressed to the head of the Jewish community in Yemen, Jacob Ben Nathaniel al-Fayyumi. For the first time in history, Yemenite Jewry was being forced to convert to Islam or be executed. The Yemenite Jews turned to the Rambam for guidance. In his letter, he told the Jews that they should convert to

Islam in order save their lives, yet practice Judaism clandestinely until the threat no longer existed and they would be able to return to the open practice of the religion.

Maimonides's life reflected the contradictions of being a Jew under Muslim rule. He was respected by Muslims, and his skill as a doctor was called upon by many powerful people. Yet his most famous practical decision on religious law involved Jews being forcibly converted to Islam. His life was shaped by having to flee from an intolerant Muslim regime, while his degree of freedom was due to living under a relatively tolerant one.

The Fatimid Dynasty

From the 10th to the latter part of the 12th century, Jews were granted religious and civil freedoms under the Fatimid caliphate in Egypt, which had adopted a policy of tolerance. Still, even here there were exceptions. Under the sixth Fatimid caliph, al-Hakim bi-Amr Allah, who ruled from 996 to 1021, this policy was abandoned. The Jews were treated as second-class citizens and subject to persecution.

This sketch depicts the Jewish philosopher and religious scholar Moses Maimonides (1135–1204). While living under Muslim rule in Egypt, Maimonides completed the Mishneh Torah, a systematic exposition of Jewish laws based on the Pentateuch and in Talmudic literature.

The Cairo Geniza, an important archive containing more than 200,000 ancient Jewish manuscripts, shows that during the Fatimid period in Egypt, the Jews played a key role in international trade. Jewish and Muslim merchants, often in partnership, traded and worked in the import and export of merchandise, including textiles, spices, fruits, and valuable metals.

The Medieval Muslim Theological Debate

During the medieval period, Muslim theologians continued to study, analyze, and interpret Islam's original texts. In an important debate between liberal and conservative interpretations, the latter won out. Regarding Jews, the former group made no innovations but the latter took an extremely negative line. This is of particular significance not only because these interpretations tended to shape thinking in later centuries—even when they had no immediate practical effect—but also because they would form the basis of 20th-century Islamist views on Jews and other non-Muslims.

Muhammad al-Ghazali

Especially important in this matter was Muhammad al-Ghazali (1058–1111), who often focused on the issue of jihad and on treatment of dhimmi peoples. According to him, Jews could be enslaved in a jihad—and these Jews would have their marriages revoked, so that married Jewish women could be taken as concubines by Muslims. Dhimmis, al-Ghazali declared, could not use the word *Allah* (which is the Arabic for God in general as well as in specific Muslim usage). He stressed that Islam mandated the humiliation to which Jews (and Christians) must be put:

> On offering up the jizya, the dhimmi must hang his head while the official takes hold of his beard and hits [the dhimmi] on the bone beneath his ear. . . . Their houses may not be higher than the Muslim's, no matter how low that is. The dhimmi may not ride an elegant horse or mule; he may ride a donkey only if the saddle is of wood. He may not walk on the good part of the road. They have to wear [an identifying] patch [on their clothing], even women, and even in the [public] baths.

While the letter of such rulings was usually not enforced, the basic themes set the tone for Muslim-Jewish relations. Jews had to be very careful to be unobtrusive in their daily lives and religious observances. Some Jewish merchants might become rich, but they faced terrible retribution if they forgot their place. This situation also ensured that Jews retained a separate identity and communal organization.

On the positive side, as long as they were careful to avoid public visibility and "minded their own business," Jews were left alone to run their own affairs and carry out their religion. The exceptions were at times of turbulence or religious extremism among Muslims, when they might be faced with physical violence or demands to convert.

There was also always the chance that the smallest incident—for example, an allegation of a single Jew insulting a Muslim or Islam as a whole—could lead to punishment or violence. Since Jews knew the rules well, had adjusted to them psychologically as well as socially, and were well aware of the huge damage that might be inflicted on them for the smallest deviation, it is reasonable to say that deliberate provocations were probably very rare. Extreme prejudice, blackmail, and personal disputes were most likely to lead to such incidents.

In a broad sense, then, the treatment of Jews by Muslims during this period was probably not extremely different from their treatment in Christian-majority countries, save only that violent incidents and physical expulsions were less frequent.

Jewish farmers harvest barley in a field near Jerusalem, early 20th century. Ottoman society considered Jews inferior to Muslims. However, despite their second-class status, Jews played an important role in commerce and trade throughout the Ottoman Empire.

Even under tolerant regimes, doctrinal anti-Jewish views might be voiced by clerics opposing more open practices. Such things happened in reaction to the two most lenient Muslim polities—in Spain and in Fatimid Egypt. This pattern could be followed even when no Jews were present. For example, the Mughal emperor Akbar in India was known for his openness to Hindu influences and for his good treatment of non-Muslim subjects. Even though these included no Jews, the 16th-century Indian Muslim theologian Ahmad Sirhindi stated that dhimmis "should constantly remain terrified and trembling. [Jizya] is intended to hold them under contempt and to uphold the honor and might of Islam." He did not refrain from adding, "Whenever a Jew is killed, it is for the benefit of Islam," though Sirhindi had no doubt never seen an actual Jew himself.

The Jews in Persia

The Persian Jewish community existed 1,000 years before the beginning of Islam. In 642, the Arab conquest reached Persia, and Islam was adopted there as the official religion. Under the Sassanid Empire, Jews had lived in relative harmony with their neighbors. Concentrated in the Zagros Mountains, Jews had enjoyed communal sovereignty, had participated in international trade and commerce, and were even permitted to hold many state positions. They did, however, suffer periodic persecution and discrimination, often at the hands of Persia's powerful Zoroastrians.

In the centuries after the Arab conquest, Jewish life in Persia was comparable to Jewish life elsewhere in the Islamic empire. The situation changed, however, after the 13th-century Mongol invasions of Persia and Iraq brought an end to the Abbasid caliphate in 1258.

The early rulers of the Il-Khanate, the Mongol state that extended across Persia and Iraq, were not Muslims. They were, in fact, hostile to Islam. These rulers respected the Jews and even offered them high-ranking positions, which did not please Muslim clerics in Persia.

In 1295, the Mongol ruler Ghazan came to the throne of the Il-Khanate. Ghazan was a Muslim, and he made Islam the official religion of his realm. Buddhists, Christians, and Jews were persecuted. While Ghazan followed the orthodox Sunni branch of Islam, he was tolerant of members of Islam's minority Shia sect. Ghazan's successor, Oljeitu, was a Shiite, and during his reign (1304–1316) Shia clerics began gaining in power.

The Tomb of Ali, an important Shiite Muslim shrine, is located in Najaf, a city in present-day Iraq. This area was once part of the Il-Khanate, the Mongol state that ruled Persia and the surrounding areas. Shia Islam became the dominant branch of the faith in this region during the period of Mongol rule in the 14th century.

Although the Il-Khanate would be destroyed before the end of the 14th century, Shia Islam became entrenched in Persia. And over the centuries, the powerful Shiite clergy sought to impose Shia Islam as the sole faith in Persia. Numerous accounts of violence against, and forcible conversion of, Persian Jews exist from the 16th century onward. For example, all the Jews in Mashhad were forced publicly to convert to Islam after a mob of Muslims rampaged through the Jewish quarter of that city in 1839. Jews in Mashhad continued practicing their faith secretly into the 20th century, however. In 1894, a massacre eliminated the entire Jewish community in Tabriz. A false rumor about the death of a young Muslim girl sparked a 1910 pogrom in the city of Shiraz; the homes and shops of Jews were looted, many Jews were killed or injured, and survivors were forced to convert to Islam.

The Ottoman Empire

The Ottoman Empire, which originated in Anatolia, was a powerful Islamic empire that lasted from the 14th century until the early 20th century. In 1453, the Ottoman Turks captured Constantinople, bringing the Byzantine Empire to an end. The Ottomans made Constantinople (which was renamed Istanbul) their capital. The Ottoman Empire rapidly expanded and within a short time came to rule over many new lands.

During the 15th and 16th centuries, there were many Jewish communities in the Ottoman Empire. Many Jews settled in Ottoman lands to escape the persecution of the Spanish Inquisition. Under Ottoman rule, the Jewish quarters were referred to as *mellahs*, and the Jews possessed basic inheritance rights.

The Ottoman leadership welcomed Jewish immigration. Jews often worked in international trade and medicine, sometimes holding important positions. Within their mellahs, the Jews were granted religious autonomy, with the chief rabbi, or *Chacham*

After the fall of Constantinople in 1453, the Ottomans converted Christian churches in the city to other uses. The Hagia Sophia—once the largest cathedral in Christendom—was converted into a mosque. However, the Jewish community flourished, with more than 40 synagogues existing in the city during the 15th and 16th centuries.

Bashi, governing on personal-status issues such as marriage and divorce. Despite these freedoms under Ottoman rule, Jews were not accepted as equals. They were subject to the dhimmi system, as were other non-Muslim groups. Eventually, additional restrictions were imposed on the Jews. These rules were a declaration of the eternal superiority of Islam and the Muslim empire. In the 16th century, relations further deteriorated between the two faiths, mainly in Shia lands, where Ottoman rule was considerably more orthodox and Jews were forced to convert to Islam.

European Dominance and the Rise of Arab Nationalism

The Crusades (late 11th century to 13th century) represented a short-term Western response to the Islamic challenge. At first these European Christian military incursions into the Muslim-controlled Holy Lands enjoyed successes, but eventually they were defeated.

In the long term, however, the balance of power shifted away from the Muslim world and to the West. This shift is attributable to a variety of factors, among the most important of which are the West's greater openness to social and ideological change, its systematic scientific research, and its broad educational opportunities, all of which led to greater technological progress. This process began with the Renaissance and continued through the

This illustrated page from a medieval French manuscript depicts European knights battling Muslims in the Holy Land. The Crusades is the name given to a series of wars fought between Christians and Muslims from 1095 to 1291.

Reformation, the conquest of the Western Hemisphere, the rise of nation-states, the end of medieval socio-political structures, and the rise of nationalism and democracy.

The Ottoman Empire reached the apex of its power during the reign of Sultan Suleyman I, known as Suleyman the Magnificent (1520–1566). In 1571, a handful of allied European states inflicted a devastating defeat on Ottoman naval forces at the Battle of Lepanto. The decisive engagement ushered in a long period of decline for the Ottoman Empire, the most powerful Muslim state.

About eighty years before the Battle of Lepanto, centuries of Muslim rule in Spain had come to an end when the Spanish monarchs King Ferdinand of Castile and Queen Isabella of Aragon conquered Granada. The fall of Granada was not simply a setback for Spain's Muslims. Jews also suffered, as Ferdinand and Isabella, who were devout Catholics, would not tolerate non-Christians in their kingdom. Thus, in 1492, Jews were ordered to convert to Christianity or be expelled immediately from Spain.

The Jews of North Africa

Thousands of Jews fled Spain rather than convert. Many settled in North Africa, where established Jewish communities already existed in Morocco, Algeria, Tunisia, and Libya. Jewish traders and merchants found work in the Mediterranean ports of these lands. The Ottoman Empire welcomed Jews, and communities developed especially in Istanbul and Salonika.

The 17th century was considered a golden age for the Jews of North Africa. Jews in Algeria, especially, became successful merchants, involved in import and export between the African ports and southern European coastal ports. Jews often worked as bazaar or long-distance merchants in the Ottoman Empire. But given both their own preferences and the Ottoman system,

Photograph of a Jewish man and woman of Jerusalem in traditional dress, from an Ottoman book published in 1873. When Jews were expelled from Spain and Portugal in the late 15th century, Sultan Beyazid II invited Jews to settle within the Ottoman Empire. Jews soon constituted a significant *millet*, or minority religious community, within the Ottoman Empire.

Jews remained a very separate community developing their own Hebrew-Arabic or Hebrew-Spanish dialect and being governed by their own religious laws.

Nevertheless, by the 19th century, persecution and pogroms against the Jews forced many to leave the Maghreb (the coastal areas of northwest Africa) in search of more peaceful surroundings. What happened to the remainder would mirror the earlier pattern in Persia. There, the Mongol conquest of an Islamic kingdom temporarily raised the status of Jews, but Muslim resentment that a dhimmi group had escaped servility led to a backlash when that group regained power. In North Africa, the granting of citizenship to Jews by the French colonial government had a similar effect.

The Crémieux Decree

Isaac Adolphe Crémieux was a French Jewish lawyer who gained considerable political influence. He wanted to help North African Jews and fought successfully to gain French citizenship for them in 1870 through a law that became known as the Décret Crémieux (the Crémieux Decree). While the decree was extremely encouraging for Algerian Jewry, it also led to increased feelings of resentment between the Jews and Muslims who, in later years, opposed the French presence.

Things went better in Egypt where, during the 19th century, a multicultural society flourished in Cairo and Alexandria. Jews played an important role in business and intellectual life and were well accepted though their numbers were relatively small. Given Egypt's orientation toward Europe and development, their role as a bridge in this direction was welcomed.

Early Arab Nationalism

In the early 20th century a great debate arose in the Muslim-majority world about how to close the gap, no longer possible to ignore, between Muslim societies and the more powerful West. Three broad orientations developed:

- to borrow and adapt Western concepts of democracy, liberalism, and modernization.

- to focus on a nationalist identity.

- to view a proper adherence to Islam—specifically, a return to what were defined as traditional Islamic virtues and loyalties—as the key to helping Muslim societies face the challenge of the West.

The problem from the standpoint of Muslim-Jewish relations is that while the first approach could succeed in integrating the two groups within a common framework, the other two approaches were disastrous in that context.

While in theory Arab, Iranian, or Turkish nationalism could have embraced Jews, in reality these ideologies (especially in the Arab case) were inextricably linked to Islam. This connection between nationalism and religion was not unique. In Europe, for example, Catholicism was integral to Polish and French national identity, and in both of these countries rising nationalism led to an increase in the persecution of Jews.

By the 19th century, it was undeniable that the Ottoman Empire—and the Muslim world in general—had fallen far behind the West economically and militarily. The Ottomans suffered a series of military setbacks, effectively ending their rule in most of central and eastern Europe. In North Africa, European colonial powers began to exert considerable influence, even in countries that remained nominally under Muslim rule. This situation generated much resentment against the ruling elite in many Muslim-majority countries, as ordinary people felt they were being simultaneously left behind, subordinated, and excluded from the benefits of Western-led modernization.

No matter what path followed, however, there was no Muslim reformation or strong secularist, anti-clerical movement to deemphasize the role of religion in polity and society as there had been in Europe. Many modernists, for example, urged that Islam be strengthened or updated in order to allow for such things as democracy and industrialization. The barriers between different religious communities never entirely came down. Though some Christian Arabs were active in variant or radical forms of Arab nationalism as a way of doing so, Jews were not attracted by such movements.

Westernizing reformers were faced with a difficult task: how to encourage Muslims to accept and embrace the modern era without alienating their audience. This task proved virtually impossible if there was any sense that the movement was against Islam or much of traditional society. At the same time, trying to justify the era of modernization through the use of Islam and Islamic ideology was also difficult, especially when faced with powerful traditionalist clerics and with popular Islamist groups.

Pan-Arabism of the 20th Century

Islam almost always served as an important common language and as a unifying force between the Muslim ruler and his Muslim subjects. Arab nationalism might battle Islamist rivals but still used Islam as a tool to reunite and revive the Arab people. In Egypt, the Wafd Party between the 1920s and 1940s was relatively secular in orientation, as was the Baath Party, mainly in Syria and Iraq, from the 1940s into the 1960s. But Islam always returned as an important component of the regime.

Despite the obstacles, Arab nationalism during the 20th century succeeded in uniting the Arab world through the idea of Pan-Arabism. To whatever extent this did or did not incorporate Islam as a central element of Arab identity, this change also created new tensions and conflict between Muslims and Jews.

Even aside from any considerations of Zionism, Jews were viewed as being affiliated with the enemy West. Another problem was that Jews were generally involved in retail and mercantile activities, and their enterprises were prime targets for nationalization by socialist-oriented Arab nationalist regimes.

In Iraq and Egypt, the Jews most prone to "assimilation" became communists, which further antagonized Arab nationalists and Muslims. In Morocco, Tunisia, and Algeria, they were French citizens, and thus at odds with the independence movements there. Even the few Jews who participated in independence struggles (mainly in Tunisia) became quickly disillusioned during the post-independence era.

The Balfour Declaration

As Arab nationalism grew stronger, so did the gap between Muslims and Jews. In 1914, in the early months of World War I, the Ottoman Empire entered the conflict on the side of Germany and Austria-Hungary and against Great Britain, France, and Russia. The British subsequently encouraged Arabs to rebel against Ottoman rule, promising to support an independent Arab state after the war. What came to be called the Arab Revolt began in 1916. The following year, the Balfour Declaration expressed, for the first time, the British government's support for the idea of a Jewish homeland in Palestine. In theory, British commitments to Arabs and to Zionists were not irreconcilable—the boundaries of potential Arab and Jewish independent states were never spelled out, and the Balfour Declaration stipulated

The Koutoubia Mosque in Marrakech, Morocco, was constructed in the 12th century. As control of North Africa passed from the Islamic Ottoman Empire to European Christians during the 18th and 19th centuries, the relationship between Muslims and Jews in North African territories became more adversarial.

that "nothing shall be done which may prejudice the civil and religious rights of existing non-Jewish communities in Palestine." Yet the competing aspirations of Arab and Jewish nationalists would lead to escalating conflict in the years between World War I and World War II.

The Zionist Movement and Its Impact

Around 1000 BCE, most of the area today known as Palestine was ruled by a powerful Jewish kingdom with its capital at Jerusalem. Over the centuries, that kingdom was divided, invaded, and conquered several times. In the process, the Jewish people became scattered across a variety of lands.

Since the second century CE, when the Romans brutally suppressed a Jewish uprising, there existed among the people of the Diaspora (Jews living outside the biblical Land of Israel, or Zion) the belief that the Jews would one day return to Zion. But the expectation was that this would happen only with the coming of the Jewish Messiah.

The Foundations of Modern Zionism

By the late 19th century, however, growing anti-Semitism in Europe, a perceived failure of assimilation, and the model of

European nationalism led Jewish intellectuals to found modern Zionism. This international political movement advocated the establishment of a Jewish national homeland.

The father of modern Zionism was a Hungarian Jewish journalist named Theodor Herzl. Herzl organized the First Zionist Congress, which was held in Basel, Switzerland, in 1897. He defined the Zionist movement's goal as striving to "create for the Jewish people, a home in Palestine secured by public law."

Theodor Herzl (1860–1904) was a Jewish journalist who lived in the Austro-Hungarian Empire. Disturbed by anti-Semitism in Europe, Herzl founded the modern Zionist movement and worked toward the establishment of a Jewish homeland.

In the first decade of the 20th century, thousands of Jews immigrated to Palestine, which was then under the control of the Ottoman Empire. The Ottoman rulers accepted these immigrants up until the outbreak of World War I, viewing them as aiding in the development of a relatively backward region of their empire and also hoping Jews would use their influence to help the Ottoman position in Europe. Early on, there was little friction between the Jewish immigrants and the Arab inhabitants of Palestine.

Arab Nationalism After the First World War

In the aftermath of World War I, the Ottoman Empire completely collapsed, and European powers were in control of large parts of the Middle East. Iraq, Jordan, Lebanon, Syria, and Palestine became British or French mandates. Egypt and the sheikdoms along the Persian Gulf were British protectorates. Algeria, Tunisia, and Morocco were French colonies, while Libya was an Italian one.

During the postwar era, Arab nationalist movements—including in Palestine—gained strength. These movements sought the creation of independent Arab states free from European domination. By the late 1920s and early 1930s, Islamism—the idea that government and society should be reordered to conform to Muslim religious law—had gained influence in Arab nationalist circles. In 1928, the Egyptian Muslim Brotherhood was founded with the goal of creating an Islamist state in Egypt and—with the foundation of branches elsewhere—other countries. In 1931, a pan-Islamic conference was held in Jerusalem; it was largely a response to a 1929 Zionist conference in Zurich, Switzerland.

Thus, opposition to Zionism came to be defined in both nationalist and religious terms. In the Islamist view Palestine, having once been conquered by Islam, must always remain in

Arab leaders gather to protest against British policies toward Jewish settlement in Palestine, circa 1929. Among the leaders is the grand mufti of Jerusalem, Amin al-Husseini (front row, second from left, wearing the white headpiece). The grand mufti's fiery rhetoric contributed to an Arab revolt in 1936–39.

Muslim hands. Explicitly in the Islamists' case, and implicitly for many Arab nationalists, Jewish inferiority was assumed, and any deviation from dhimmi status had to be severely punished.

While incidents of Zionist–Arab Palestinian violence occurred throughout the 1920s and early 1930s, the real turning point was the 1936 general strike of Arabs in Palestine followed by the diplomatic intervention of Arab regimes and an uprising that started in 1937. Not only Jews but also the British and Arabs of the opposition faction came under attack. The fact that the leader of the Arab uprising was Amin al-Husseini, the grand mufti of Jerusalem (the highest-ranking Muslim religious figure in Palestine), intensified the religious dimension. Husseini fled first to Iraq and later to Germany, where he spent World War II cooperating with the Nazi regime.

Through the 1930s, however, Jews in Muslim-majority countries were relatively little touched by the conflict in Palestine. There were two major reasons for this. First, where the British or French were in control of Arab countries, they prevented Arab-Jewish violence. Second, Arab and Muslim-majority states were generally governed by more moderate traditionalist, modernizing, or somewhat secular-minded regimes. In Turkey, the secular-oriented nationalist regime of Kemal Ataturk and in Iran the modernizing government of the shah were little interested in the Palestine issue and also kept down radical nationalist or Islamist forces.

The "Farhud" in Iraq

Iraq was the first country where radical Arab nationalists came to power. In April 1941, during World War II, the nationalist politician Rashid Ali al-Gailani, backed by four important army officers, took control of the Iraqi government in a coup. The new regime was pro-Germany, and the British quickly moved to eliminate a potentially valuable ally of its wartime enemy. In mid-April, a British task force from India landed in southern Iraq while British-commanded soldiers from the army of Transjordan swept into the country from the west. By late May, with British forces near the outskirts of Baghdad, the regime had collapsed. Ali al-Gailani and the other coup leaders fled Iraq, ultimately finding refuge in Germany.

Arguably, Iraq had been the Arab country where Muslim-Jewish relations had been best. The Jewish community had been there for centuries, was economically integrated, and had never had any direct political involvement with European powers.

Nevertheless, on June 1–2, 1941, anti-Jewish rioting known as the *Farhud* ("pogrom") ripped through Baghdad. The violence was encouraged by supporters of Ali al-Gailani and Iraqi radical nationalists who regarded the Jews as collaborators with British colonial authorities. But at its heart the Farhud was simply a manifestation of deep-seated anti-Semitism—though it must be noted that some Muslims hid their Jewish neighbors during the violence. Still, between 150 and 180 Jews were killed during the two-day rampage, and an estimated 600 others were injured. In addition, more than 1,500 Jewish-owned businesses and homes were looted.

The Pogrom in Aden

After World War II ended in 1945, there were about 8,000 Jews living in Aden, which was then a British colony. In late 1947, however, three days of anti-Jewish rioting erupted in Aden. At least 82 Jews were killed and hundreds were injured, four synagogues in the city were destroyed, and hundreds of Jewish homes and businesses were looted.

The catalyst for the pogrom in Aden—as well as violence in other cities across the Middle East (most notably Aleppo, Syria)—was the November 29, 1947, United Nations vote to partition British-mandate Palestine. The UN plan, which would create an Arab state and a Jewish state, was to go into effect in 1948, when the British withdrew from Palestine. But while the Zionist leadership accepted the partition, the Palestinian leadership did not. Almost immediately, Palestinians launched attacks against Jews. Zionists retaliated with attacks against Palestinians. Soon Palestine was engulfed in a brutal civil war.

(Top) Andrei I. Gromyko, representing the Soviet Union, speaks in support of a United Nations proposal to partition Palestine into Jewish and Arab states, November 29, 1947. The UN General Assembly approved the partition proposal by a vote of 33 to 13, with 10 abstentions and one absence. (Right) Speaking beneath a large portrait of Theodor Herzl, David Ben-Gurion declares Israel's independence in Tel Aviv, May 14, 1948.

The Zionists suffered setbacks early on. But in April 1948, they launched a successful offensive and seized control of strategic territory. On May 14, 1948, as the British presence in Palestine officially ended, Zionists proclaimed the establishment of the State of Israel. The armies of five Arab states invaded, but Israel fought them off. By early 1949, Israel had expanded the territory it controlled well beyond the original partition boundaries. The Palestinian Arabs, meanwhile, were left without a state, as Transjordan (later Jordan) occupied the West Bank territory and East Jerusalem, and Egypt was in control of the Gaza Strip.

Over the next decade, the overwhelming majority of Jews left Muslim-majority countries for Israel. The long presence of Jews in those places was almost totally ended.

Conclusions

Muslim-Jewish relations have been the subject of much study—and much controversy. Many people are inclined to reduce the 1,300-year history of Muslim-Jewish interactions to a simplistic narrative that supports a particular political or ideological agenda. But the reality is that Muslim-Jewish relations have varied greatly by place and time.

Nonetheless, certain generalizations are useful. To begin, the normative Islamic conception of Jews and their status under Muslim rule was as a subordinate dhimmi population. Protection was purchased with submission. While the People of the Book were given higher status than pagans, they were also seen as inferior, both in political status and spiritual correctness. There is support for this doctrine in Muslim sacred texts.

Nonetheless, for long periods the details of this doctrine were ignored. Under Muslim rule at certain times and in certain places, individual Jews could—and did—achieve wealth and high rank, and Jewish communities flourished. Examples include Spain, Fatimid Egypt, and the Ottoman Empire. At other times and in other places, however, Jews were persecuted. Some of the worst mistreatment of Jews occurred in seventh-century Arabia and in Persia.

While the overall incidence of active persecution and forced conversion of Jews was lower in Muslim lands than in Christian Europe, the basic pattern was parallel. The key factor related to the dominant view of the ruling government. Regimes that relaxed the strictness of religious observance or were somewhat heterodox in their own right tended to be more lenient toward Jews. Regimes that were more puritanical in their views enforced restrictions more tightly.

As political modernization set in, this measurement came to apply to political movements regardless of their piety. As in Europe, the definition of Jews changed from strictly religious to national. That is, in medieval Europe, Jews were seen as nonbelievers who lay outside the dominant community, which itself was defined in religious terms. In Muslim-majority countries, the same applied.

However, as nationalism developed in Europe, Jews were defined as "the other" in ethnic-communal terms. They were not proper Poles or Frenchmen, for example, partly because such a person would have to be a Catholic, partly on ethnic-historical terms. In Europe, however, liberalism and moderate definitions of nationalism, at least from about the mid-19th century onward, fostered more inclusive definitions of nationality. Yet even in Europe, these were opposed and often lost out—at least for long periods of time—to harder-line views.

The Muslim-majority world followed a similar pattern, with two notable exceptions. Religious definitions of community remained stronger, and liberalism was almost nonexistent. Jews

Although Jews lived in peace under Muslim rule at many times and places throughout history, the Qur'an, Islam's holy scriptures, includes many verses that criticize Jews for not following the teachings of Muhammad.

were consistently defined as outside the Islamic and Arab national communities. A change in the Jews' dhimmi status was seen as unacceptable according to Islam, and this view was often present implicitly in Arab nationalist doctrine.

Zionism and the creation of Israel did play a major role in stirring up antagonism toward, and violence against, Jewish communities in Muslim-majority countries. Yet this role should not be overstated. Arguably, a strain of anti-Semitism always existed in Islam. After all, a well-known hadith (Sahih 41, 6985) says that on Judgment Day, "The Muslims will fight the Jews who will hide behind rocks and trees. The rocks and trees will cry out: O Muslim! A Jew is hiding behind me. Come kill him."

The brief story is that the Jews were generally left alone in Muslim-majority states, periodically persecuted, and not at all integrated in any social or political way. But the evolution that took place in much of the West—toward full citizenship and a definition of nationality and citizenship totally divorced from religion—never happened in Muslim-majority countries.

Chronology

570: The prophet Muhammad, Islam's founder, is born in Mecca.

610: Muhammad, Muslims believe, receives his first revelation from Allah, delivered by the angel Gabriel.

622: Muhammad and a few hundred followers are forced to leave Mecca; they settle in Medina, where Muhammad attempts to gain the support of the Jewish tribes and create a community constitution.

628: The Banu Qurayza massacre takes place in Medina.

630: Mecca surrenders to Muhammad and his followers.

632: Muhammad dies, and Arab Muslim conquests begin.

711: Beginning of the Muslim conquest of the Iberian Peninsula.

909: Egypt comes under the rule of the Fatimid dynasty.

1066: A great number of Jews are put to death in Granada, Spain, following the alleged disloyalty of Joseph ibn Nagrela, a Jewish minister of the king.

1172: Moses Maimonides writes the famous "Epistle to the Jews in Yemen," advising them to convert temporarily to Islam in order to save their lives.

1219: Mongol forces invade Persia.

1258: Mongols conquer Baghdad and bring an end to the Abbasid caliphate.

Early 14th century: Beginnings of the Ottoman Empire.

1453: Ottomans conquer Constantinople, bringing the Byzantine Empire to an end.

1492: Following the Christian reconquest of Iberia, the Spanish monarchs order Jews either to convert to Christianity or be expelled immediately from Spain.

1870: The Décret Crémieux becomes law; it secures French citizenship for the Jews in Algeria.

1881: The beginning of "Aliya," in which Jews in the Diaspora migrate to Palestine, which they regard as their biblical homeland.

1894: A pogrom in Tabriz, Persia, eliminates most of the Jewish community in the city.

1897: The First Zionist Conference is held in Basel, Switzerland.

1910: Pogrom in the city of Shiraz, Persia.

1917: The Balfour Declaration commits Britain to supporting the establishment of a Jewish homeland in Palestine.

1918: The Ottoman Empire collapses.

1921: Faisal becomes king of Iraq and Jews are made equal citizens of the new state.

1928: The Muslim Brotherhood is founded in Egypt by Hasan al-Banna; branches in other countries are later formed.

1931: The General Islamic Conference brings together nationalist activists from all Arab countries; they seek to maintain Muslim control over Jerusalem and prevent the establishment of a Jewish state.

1936: The Arab Revolt targets Jews, British officials, and dissident Arabs in British-ruled mandatory Palestine.

1941: The Farhud, anti-Jewish rioting in Baghdad, leaves up to 180 Jews dead.

1945: World War II ends and the United Nations is formed.

1947: The United Nations votes for the partition of Palestine; this event provokes huge, sometimes violent demonstrations throughout the Middle East, including a pogrom in Aden.

1948: The State of Israel is established on May 14.

A view of the Dome of the Rock, Jerusalem. Built between 688 and 691 CE, the Islamic shrine sits atop the Temple Mount, land that is sacred to the Jews.

Glossary

caliph—a title given to the successors of Muhammad as the spiritual and political leader of Sunni Islam; in the Ottoman Empire, the sultan held the title of caliph.

dhimmi—a social status forced upon followers of monotheistic religions (other than Islam) who lived under Muslim rule. The dhimmi status obligated non-Muslim subjects to pay a high tax known as jizyah.

Diaspora—the Jews living outside Palestine or modern Israel.

Hadith—Collected sayings or traditions of the prophet Muhammad and his close companions, which for centuries have been regarded as lines of guidance for Muslims.

jihad—a "holy war" waged by Muslims on behalf of Islam.

Maghreb—a region of northwest Africa that includes the Mediterranean coastal areas of Morocco, Algeria, and Tunisia (and sometimes Libya); the term is also sometimes used to refer to these countries in their entirety.

Pan-Arabism—a movement or ideology seeking the political union of all Arab nations.

pogrom—an organized massacre, especially of Jews.

Qur'an—Islam's holy scriptures, a key source of Islamic law and practice.

Shia—the smaller of Islam's two major branches, whose rift with the larger Sunni branch originated with seventh-century disputes over who should succeed the prophet

Muhammad as leader of the Muslim community. The Shia branch makes up the majority of people in Iran, Iraq, and Bahrain and is the largest single communal group in Lebanon.

Zionism—the modern national movement of the Jewish people.

Zoroastrians—followers of a monotheistic Persian religion founded in the sixth century BCE, which holds that the Supreme God, Ahura Mazda, is locked in a struggle against the evil spirit Ahriman and requires the good deeds of humans to aid him in this struggle.

The Cave of the Patriarchs in Hebron. Tradition holds that it contains the tombs of the Jewish people's patriarchs and matriarchs, including Adam and Eve, Abraham and Sarah, Isaac and Rebekah, and Jacob and Leah. The site is also revered by Muslims, who call it the Ibrahimi Mosque.

Further Reading

Bostom, Andrew. *The Legacy of Islamic Anti-Semitism: From Sacred Texts to Solemn History*. Amherst, N.Y.: Prometheus Books, 2008.

———. *The Legacy of Jihad: Islamic Holy War and the Fate of Non-Muslims*. Amherst, N.Y.: Prometheus Books, 2008.

Brinner, William M., et al. (editors). *Judaism and Islam, Boundaries, Communication and Interaction*. Leiden, Netherlands, and Boston: Brill, 2000.

Cohen, Mark. *Under Crescent and Cross: The Jews in the Middle Ages*. Princeton, N.J.: Princeton University Press, 1995.

Hirschberg, Haim Zeev; Eliezer Bashan; and Robert Attal. *A History of the Jews in North Africa*. Leiden, Netherlands, and Boston: Brill, 1981.

Hourani, Albert. *A History of the Arab Peoples* (London: Faber and Faber, 1991).

Ibn Ishaq, M. *The Life of Muhammad: A Translation of Ishaq's Sirat Rasul Allah*, translated by Alfred A. Guillaume (Karachi: Oxford University Press, 1996).

Kedar, Mordechai. *Asad in Search of Legitimacy: Message and Rhetoric in the Syrian Press Under Hafiz and Bashar*. Sussex, UK: Sussex Academic Press, 2006.

Laqueur, Walter, and Barry Rubin. *The Israel-Arab Reader: A Documentary History of the Middle East Conflict*. New York: Penguin Books, 2001.

Lewis, Bernard. *The Arabs in History*. New York: Oxford University Press, 1950.

Nasr-Abun, Jamil M. *A History of the Maghreb in the Islamic Period*. Cambridge, UK: Cambridge University Press, 1987.

Nettler, Ronald. *Medieval and Modern Perspectives on Muslim-Jewish Relations*. London: Routledge, 1995.

Porter, Ruth, and Sarah Harel-Hoshen (editors). *Odyssey of the Exiles: The Sephardi Jews 1492–1992*. Tel Aviv: Ministry of Defense Publishing House, 1992.

Spyer, Jonathan, and Cameron Brown. *The Rise of Nationalism: The Arab World, Turkey and Iran*. Philadelphia: Mason Crest Publishers, 2008.

Stillman, Norman. *Jews of Arab Lands: A History and Source Book*. Philadelphia: Jewish Publication Society, 1979.

Internet Resources

http://memri.org

> The Middle East Media Research Institute (MEMRI) Web site offers translations of international news and academic articles from the region.

http://www.arabworldnews.com

> Provides news and information from the World News network for the Arab world.

http://www.meriajournal.com

> *The Middle East Review of International Affairs (MERIA) Journal* offers scholarly articles on a wide variety of topics affecting the region and the world.

Index

Numbers in **bold italics** refer to captions.